Travel Guide to Heidelberg 2024

A Comprehensive Traveler's Guide to Unraveling Historic Beauty

By

JASON TERRY

Table of contents

Conclusion

Introduction

Nestled along the serene banks of the Neckar River, Heidelberg stands as a timeless gem in the heart of southwestern Germany, adorned with an enigmatic blend of history, culture, and picturesque landscapes. This city, with its cobblestone streets and architectural marvels, invites visitors to step into a narrative woven over centuries, where each alleyway whispers tales of antiquity.

Heidelberg's story dates back to the early days of the Holy Roman Empire, tracing its origins to the 5th century when a modest settlement emerged on the banks of the Neckar. However, it was in the late Middle Ages that the city flourished, becoming a pivotal center of learning and culture in Europe. Renowned for the establishment of Heidelberg University in 1386, the city became a beacon of intellectual pursuit, attracting scholars and thinkers from across the continent.

Yet, Heidelberg's allure extends beyond academia. Its historical narrative is intertwined with the tumultuous events of wars and transitions, notably during the Thirty Years' War and subsequent conflicts, which left an indelible mark on its landscape. The iconic Heidelberg Castle, a magnificent red sandstone edifice perched atop the Königstuhl hill, bears witness to these chapters of triumph and turmoil. Its weathered walls echo the whispers of the past, standing as a testament to the city's resilience.

Heidelberg, though steeped in history, pulsates with a modern vibrancy that harmoniously complements its antique charm. The city's cobbled streets adorned with half-timbered houses exude an old-world charm that captivates visitors, while the bustling Marktplatz serves as a hub for social gatherings and cultural celebrations.

The spirit of Heidelberg transcends its architectural splendor. It reverberates through the city's diverse cultural offerings, from world-class museums and theaters to lively festivals that enchant both locals and tourists alike. Whether immersed in the artistic wonders at the Kurpfälzisches Museum or savoring a performance at the Heidelberg Theater, visitors find themselves enveloped in a cultural tapestry that embodies the essence of the city.

Heidelberg's allure lies not only in its historical grandeur but also in the profound inspirations it bestows upon those who traverse its winding streets. The Philosophers' Walk, a scenic trail on the northern banks of the Neckar, has been a muse for poets, writers, and thinkers for centuries. The panoramic views of the city below, coupled with the tranquil ambiance, offer solace and stimulate the creative soul.

As the sun sets behind the silhouette of the castle, Heidelberg transforms into a canvas painted with hues of warmth and enchantment. The city's mystical aura takes hold, captivating the hearts of all who wander its lanes.

In this comprehensive traveler's guide, we invite you to embark on a journey through the centuries, as we unravel the layers of Heidelberg's historic beauty and present-day splendor. Join us in exploring the city's treasures, embracing its culture, and discovering the magic that makes Heidelberg an unforgettable destination.

Heidelberg's allure is not confined solely to its historical legacy; it thrives on the amalgamation of diverse influences that have shaped its character. The city's narrative unfolds through the lens of various epochs, each leaving its mark on the architecture, customs, and traditions. From the Roman foundations to the Renaissance and Baroque embellishments, Heidelberg embodies a mosaic of styles that showcase the city's evolution over centuries.

At the heart of this cultural confluence lies Heidelberg University, a bastion of knowledge and innovation. The university's esteemed reputation and intellectual prowess have fostered an environment that continues to attract inquisitive minds from around the world. Its illustrious alumni, including Nobel laureates and eminent scholars, have contributed significantly to the city's intellectual legacy.

The pulse of Heidelberg resonates through its enchanting Old Town, a labyrinth of narrow streets adorned with charming cafés, boutique shops, and historic landmarks. Strolling through the Hauptstraße, one of Europe's longest pedestrian streets, offers a delightful experience where history intertwines with the contemporary. Visitors are beckoned to explore hidden courtyards, visit quaint bookstores, or simply indulge in a cup of coffee while admiring the architectural splendor surrounding them.

One of the most iconic sights along this ancient thoroughfare is the Heiliggeistkirche (Church of the Holy Spirit), an architectural masterpiece that stands as a symbol of Heidelberg's religious heritage. Its elegant façade and captivating interiors resonate with the echoes of centuries-old prayers and celebrations.

Heidelberg's allure extends beyond its architectural treasures. Nature, too, plays a vital role in the city's charm. The Neckar River meanders gracefully through the city, offering scenic vistas and a tranquil ambiance. Visitors often find respite along its banks, indulging in leisurely boat rides or simply admiring the reflections of the city's skyline on its shimmering waters.

The verdant landscapes surrounding Heidelberg are equally captivating. The city is embraced by lush hillsides adorned with verdant vineyards, offering panoramic views that mesmerize visitors and locals alike. These landscapes, changing hues with the seasons, add another layer of enchantment to the city's allure.

Heidelberg's charm doesn't solely rest upon its architectural marvels and historical significance; it's the warmth of its people that completes the tapestry of experiences. The friendly locals, known for their hospitality, eagerly share stories of their beloved city, recommend hidden gems, and extend a welcoming hand to those who venture into their midst.

In "Heidelberg Unveiled: A Comprehensive Traveler's Guide to Unraveling Historic Beauty," we endeavor to encapsulate the essence of this captivating city, guiding travelers through its myriad offerings, from historical landmarks to cultural experiences and beyond. Join us as we unravel the layers of Heidelberg's beauty and create memories that will linger long after the journey concludes.

Chapter 1: Planning Your Trip

Travel Essentials: What to Know Before You Go

Before embarking on your journey to Heidelberg, it's crucial to be well-prepared. Ensure your passport is valid, and if you require a visa, make sure to obtain it in advance. Familiarize yourself with the local currency (Euro) and have some cash on hand for initial expenses. The official language is German, so having a few basic phrases can be immensely helpful.

Heidelberg enjoys a temperate climate, but weather can vary. Pack accordingly, including comfortable walking shoes, as exploring the city often involves strolling through cobblestone streets and hilly terrains. Don't forget to bring layers, as temperatures can fluctuate. Also, having a universal adapter for electrical outlets is advisable.

Best Times to Visit Heidelberg

Heidelberg boasts its charm throughout the year, each season offering a unique allure. Spring (April to June) brings blooming flowers, pleasant temperatures, and fewer crowds, making it an ideal time for sightseeing and outdoor activities. Summer (July to August) is peak tourist season, characterized by vibrant festivals and lively events. The warm weather encourages al fresco dining and leisurely river cruises.

Autumn (September to November) paints the city in golden hues, with mild weather and the grape harvest season adding a touch of romance to Heidelberg's ambiance. Winter (December to February) offers a quieter atmosphere, adorned with festive decorations and Christmas markets. While it might be chilly, the enchanting winter scenes and fewer tourists create a serene experience.

Travel Itinerary Suggestions for Different Durations

1-2 Days:

Day 1: Explore the Old Town, visit the Heidelberg Castle, stroll along the Hauptstraße, and enjoy a scenic Neckar River cruise.

Day 2: Discover the Philosophers' Walk, visit museums like the Kurpfälzisches Museum, and savor local cuisine at traditional restaurants.
3-4 Days:

Day 3: Venture beyond Heidelberg for a day trip to nearby towns such as Schwetzingen or Ladenburg.
Day 4: Engage in outdoor activities like hiking in the surrounding hills or take a wine tasting tour in the nearby vineyards.

5-7 Days:
Extend your exploration with more in-depth visits to historical sites, attend cultural events or take cooking classes to immerse yourself in the local culture.
Consider exploring farther regions of the Rhine-Neckar Metropolitan Region for a diverse experience.

By understanding the travel essentials, choosing the best time to visit Heidelberg based on your preferences, and tailoring your itinerary to the duration of your stay, you'll be better equipped to maximize your experience in this captivating city.

Heidelberg's timeless charm and diverse offerings ensure an unforgettable journey, no matter the season or the length of your stay.

Besides the fundamental necessities, consider obtaining a Heidelberg Card or City Pass upon arrival. These cards offer discounts on attractions, public transportation, and sometimes even free entry to certain museums or tours, making them a cost-effective choice for exploring the city.

Ensure you have comprehensive travel insurance to cover any unexpected situations, including medical emergencies and trip cancellations. Familiarize yourself with the local transportation system, including buses, trams, and the convenient funicular railway to the castle, enabling smooth navigation around the city.

Research local customs and etiquette to ensure respectful interactions. Tipping in Germany isn't obligatory but appreciated, usually rounding up to the nearest Euro for good service at restaurants or leaving a small tip for taxi drivers.

Fine-Tuning Your Visit: Best Times for Specific Interests

The timing of your visit can cater to specific interests. For instance, if you're a photography enthusiast, the golden hues of autumn offer stunning vistas for capturing the city's beauty. Art aficionados might consider visiting during the annual Heidelberg Spring Exhibition or enjoying open-air concerts during the summer.

Food enthusiasts can plan their visit around the Heidelberg Gourmet Festival in late autumn, indulging in culinary delights and wine tastings. Winter enthusiasts, on the other hand, can revel in the festive atmosphere of the Christmas markets, sipping on glühwein (mulled wine) and enjoying seasonal treats.

Tailoring Itineraries for Personal Preferences

Customize your itinerary based on personal interests. If history fascinates you, allocate more time to delve into the Heidelberg Castle's rich history, or perhaps plan visits to the Studentenkarzer

(Student Prison) and the Church of the Holy Spirit to absorb different historical facets.

Nature enthusiasts might extend their time exploring the trails around Heidelberg, like the Philosopher's Walk or the Neckar Valley Cycle Path, immersing themselves in the region's natural beauty. Alternatively, consider engaging in local workshops or cultural experiences to gain a deeper understanding of Heidelberg's traditions and crafts.

Blending Exploration with Serendipity

While it's valuable to plan ahead, leave room for spontaneity. Wander the streets without a set agenda, stumble upon hidden alleyways adorned with street art, or strike up conversations with locals at cozy cafes. Sometimes, the most memorable experiences arise from unplanned moments.

By combining practical preparation, aligning the visit with personal interests, and allowing space for serendipitous encounters, travelers can create a balanced and enriching experience in Heidelberg, embracing both the planned and the unexpected elements that the city has to offer.

Chapter 2: Exploring Heidelberg

The Old Town Charm: Exploring Altstadt's Historic Streets

Heidelberg's Altstadt, or Old Town, is an enchanting labyrinth of cobblestone streets, charming squares, and historic buildings that exude an aura of centuries past. Wander through the Hauptstraße, one of Europe's longest pedestrian streets, where each step unveils architectural wonders, inviting cafés, and boutique shops.

The town's focal point is the Marktplatz, a bustling square framed by the Town Hall (Rathaus) and the Church of the Holy Spirit (Heiliggeistkirche). The church's stunning red sandstone façade and its interiors adorned with intricate details reflect the city's rich religious heritage.

As you stroll through the maze of alleys, you'll encounter the delightful Carl Theodor Old Bridge (Alte Brücke), offering panoramic views of the castle and the river. Adjacent to the bridge lies the historic Neckar Gate (Neckartor), a vestige of the city's medieval fortifications.

The Altstadt's charm lies not only in its architectural splendor but also in its inviting atmosphere. Stop by a traditional Konditorei (pastry shop) to indulge in a slice of the famous Heidelberg almond cake or explore local artisan stores offering unique crafts and souvenirs.

Heidelberg Castle: A Historical Icon and its Surrounding Gardens
Perched majestically atop the Königstuhl hill, the Heidelberg Castle stands as a testament to the city's rich history and resilience. This iconic castle, a blend of Gothic and Renaissance architecture, holds within its walls centuries of triumphs, tragedies, and architectural evolution.

While exploring the castle ruins, visitors are immersed in its compelling narrative. Marvel at the impressive Friedrich Building, the stunning Renaissance courtyard, and the atmospheric Great Barrel, one of the largest wine barrels in the world. From the terrace, soak in panoramic vistas of

Heidelberg's skyline and the Neckar River winding through the valley.

Adjacent to the castle lies the idyllic Hortus Palatinus, or Garden of the Palatinate, offering a serene escape. These terraced gardens, once a masterpiece of Renaissance landscaping, have been partially restored, showcasing vibrant floral displays, enchanting sculptures, and tranquil pathways.

Philosophers' Walk: Stunning Views and Riverside Beauty

For a serene escape and breathtaking vistas, venture to the Philosophers' Walk (Philosophenweg). This scenic trail on the northern banks of the Neckar River offers a leisurely stroll through verdant hillsides and offers panoramic views of Heidelberg's Old Town and the Neckar Valley below.

Immerse yourself in the serene ambiance as you follow the footsteps of philosophers and scholars who sought inspiration along this picturesque route. The tranquil setting, complemented by the gentle rustling of leaves and the meandering river below, provides a space for contemplation and relaxation.

Neckar River Cruises: Exploring Heidelberg from the Water

To experience Heidelberg from a different perspective, embark on a leisurely Neckar River cruise. Drift along the water, passing under the iconic Old Bridge, while enjoying stunning views of the castle perched on the hilltop and the picturesque cityscape along the riverbanks.

These cruises offer a tranquil retreat, allowing visitors to soak in the city's beauty while learning about its history from knowledgeable guides. Enjoy the serenity of the water, capturing postcard-worthy views and discovering hidden angles of Heidelberg that are only visible from the Neckar.

Chapter 3: Experiencing Culture and Entertainment

Museums: Begin your cultural journey at the Kurpfälzisches Museum, housing a treasure trove of artifacts that narrate the region's history. Delve into art, archaeology, and local heritage through its captivating exhibitions. For art enthusiasts, the Heidelberg Art Association (Kunstverein) presents contemporary artworks by both local and international artists.

The Deutsches Apotheken Museum (German Pharmacy Museum) within Heidelberg Castle showcases the evolution of pharmaceuticals, providing insights into centuries-old medical practices. Science enthusiasts will find the German Cancer Research Center (Deutsches Krebsforschungszentrum) intriguing, offering informative exhibits on cancer research and therapies.

Theaters and Concerts: Heidelberg's cultural tapestry is woven with vibrant theater productions and captivating musical performances. The

Heidelberg Theater (Theater Heidelberg) stages a diverse repertoire of plays, operas, and ballets throughout the year, showcasing both classic and contemporary works.

For music aficionados, the city hosts a myriad of concerts across genres. The Philharmonisches Orchester Heidelberg (Heidelberg Philharmonic Orchestra) and the Heidelberger Frühling festival celebrate classical music, attracting renowned musicians and orchestras from around the world.

Festivals and Events: Celebrating Heidelberg's Vibrant Spirit

Heidelberg pulsates with energy during its numerous festivals and events that celebrate art, culture, and local traditions throughout the year.

The Heidelberg Spring Festival (Heidelberger Frühling) is a highlight, enchanting visitors with a month-long celebration of classical music, featuring concerts, recitals, and masterclasses held at various venues across the city. In summer, the Castle Illuminations (Schlossbeleuchtung) transform

Heidelberg Castle into a mesmerizing spectacle of light and fireworks, commemorating historic events.

The Heidelberg Literature Days (Heidelberger Literaturtage) attract literary enthusiasts, offering readings, discussions, and book presentations by acclaimed authors. Wine lovers should not miss the Heidelberg Castle Wine Festival (Heidelberger Schlossfestspiele), where regional wineries showcase their finest vintages amid a backdrop of castle splendor.

Nightlife and Dining: Savory Delights and Evening Entertainment

Heidelberg's nightlife seamlessly blends with its culinary delights, offering a spectrum of dining experiences and evening entertainment.

The Old Town buzzes with bars, pubs, and cocktail lounges catering to diverse tastes. From traditional German beer gardens to chic rooftop bars, the city offers venues for socializing and unwinding. Enjoy a glass of locally brewed beer or sip on regional wines while soaking in the vibrant ambiance of the city's nightlife.

For culinary exploration, Heidelberg boasts a myriad of restaurants offering a fusion of flavors. Sample traditional German cuisine at rustic taverns or indulge in gourmet dining at Michelin-starred establishments. The city's diverse culinary landscape accommodates all palates, with international eateries, vegetarian/vegan options, and trendy cafes serving artisanal treats.

After a satisfying meal, immerse yourself in the city's evening entertainment. Live music venues, jazz clubs, and theaters host performances that cater to varying tastes. The HipHop Garden, Karlstorbahnhof, and Halle02 are venues where you can groove to live music or dance the night away.

Cultural Workshops and Art Galleries

Beyond museums and theaters, Heidelberg offers engaging cultural workshops and art galleries that allow visitors to actively participate and appreciate local artistry. Consider attending pottery classes, painting workshops, or even glassblowing sessions, where skilled artisans impart their expertise, providing hands-on experiences for all ages.

Art galleries, such as the Heidelberg Gallery Association (Galerieverein), display a diverse array of contemporary art, showcasing the talents of local and international artists. These galleries often host exhibitions, artist talks, and workshops, offering a deeper understanding of the creative processes behind the artworks.

Cultural Heritage Walks and Guided Tours

Immerse yourself in Heidelberg's cultural heritage by joining themed walks or guided tours that focus on specific aspects of the city's history, architecture, or cultural significance. Expert guides lead tours through lesser-known alleys, historic buildings, and hidden landmarks, revealing captivating stories and anecdotes that breathe life into the city's past.

From literary tours exploring Heidelberg's connection to famous poets like Goethe and Mark Twain to themed walks exploring the Jewish Quarter's history, these guided experiences provide a deeper appreciation for the city's multifaceted cultural heritage.

Unique Dining Experiences

Heidelberg's culinary landscape extends beyond traditional dining; it offers unique experiences that combine food, history, and entertainment. Consider a dinner cruise on the Neckar River, indulging in gourmet cuisine while admiring the city's illuminated skyline from the water.

For a taste of authenticity, join local food tours that traverse hidden culinary gems, introducing visitors to regional specialties and family-owned eateries. These tours offer insights into local gastronomy while providing an opportunity to interact with passionate chefs and food artisans.

Eclectic Nightlife Venues

Heidelberg's nightlife caters to a diverse audience, offering an eclectic mix of venues to suit different preferences. Dive into the city's alternative scene by exploring underground clubs hosting indie music bands, experimental performances, and themed parties that foster a unique and vibrant atmosphere.

Those seeking a relaxed evening can opt for cozy wine bars or intimate jazz lounges that offer a laid-back ambiance, perfect for unwinding after a day of exploration. Many venues also feature live music sessions showcasing local talents across various genres, ensuring there's something for every music enthusiast.

Cultural Fusion and Community Events

Heidelberg's cultural fabric is interwoven with a rich tapestry of diverse communities. Embrace cultural fusion by attending community events that celebrate diversity, from international food festivals to cultural showcases highlighting traditions from around the world.

Participate in community-driven initiatives, such as language exchange meetups, art exhibitions celebrating cultural diversity, or intercultural workshops that foster dialogue and understanding among different communities residing in Heidelberg.

Cultural Enclaves and Artisanal Markets

Heidelberg's cultural diversity is evident in its vibrant enclaves and artisanal markets. Wander through multicultural districts like the Weststadt, where diverse communities coalesce, creating an atmosphere brimming with international flavors, music, and art. Engage with locals, taste global cuisines, and discover unique crafts that reflect the city's cosmopolitan essence.

Artisanal markets, such as the weekly Saturday market at Kornmarkt, offer a feast for the senses. Delight in the colorful stalls brimming with fresh produce, local delicacies, handcrafted goods, and aromatic flowers. It's not just a marketplace; it's a celebration of Heidelberg's agricultural heritage and craftsmanship.

Interactive Cultural Performances and Street Art
Immerse yourself in interactive cultural performances that transcend traditional theater experiences. Participatory events, immersive theater, and street performances unfold in unexpected corners of Heidelberg, inviting spectators to become part of the narrative. Engage in live storytelling, street art exhibitions, or pop-up performances that bring the city's streets alive with creativity.

Explore Heidelberg's vibrant street art scene by taking guided tours or self-guided walks through neighborhoods adorned with colorful murals, graffiti art, and thought-provoking installations. These urban artworks often convey powerful messages, serving as a canvas for social commentary and artistic expression.

Seasonal Celebrations and Local Traditions

Heidelberg's cultural calendar is enriched with seasonal celebrations and age-old traditions that encapsulate the spirit of the city. Dive into the festive atmosphere during the Christmas season, when the city transforms into a winter wonderland adorned with twinkling lights, enchanting markets, and traditional crafts. Experience the magical Heidelberg Christmas Market, where the aroma of roasted chestnuts and mulled wine fills the air.

Experience local traditions like Fasching (Carnival) or the Heidelberger Herbst (Heidelberg Autumn) festival, celebrating the changing seasons with vibrant parades, folk music, and culinary delights. These events offer a glimpse into the community's heritage, fostering a sense of unity and shared celebration.

Culinary Experiments and Gastronomic Adventures:

Heidelberg's culinary scene continually evolves, offering opportunities for gastronomic adventures and culinary experiments. Embark on themed dining experiences that merge food, history, and storytelling, such as medieval feasts or themed dinners inspired by literary works associated with the city.

For culinary enthusiasts seeking hands-on experiences, consider participating in cooking classes or workshops led by local chefs. Learn the secrets behind regional specialties, participate in wine tasting sessions, or try your hand at crafting traditional German dishes, creating lasting memories of your Heidelberg visit.

Chapter 4: Accommodation Options

Types of Accommodation: Hotels, Guesthouses, and Unique Stays
Heidelberg offers a diverse range of accommodations catering to various preferences and budgets.

Hotels: From luxurious five-star establishments to boutique hotels and comfortable mid-range options, Heidelberg's hotels provide a range of amenities and services. These accommodations often feature convenient locations, impeccable service, and amenities such as spas, restaurants, and concierge services, catering to travelers seeking comfort and convenience.

Guesthouses and Bed & Breakfasts: For a more intimate experience, consider staying in charming guesthouses or bed & breakfasts scattered throughout the city. These accommodations often offer personalized service, cozy rooms, and the opportunity to interact closely with local hosts, providing a homely ambiance and insights into the city's culture.

Unique Stays: Heidelberg also boasts unique and unconventional accommodations, such as historical mansions turned into boutique hotels, castle hotels, or even houseboats along the Neckar River. These distinctive stays offer an unforgettable experience, allowing guests to immerse themselves in the city's history or natural surroundings.

Neighborhood Insights: Best Areas to Stay in Heidelberg
Altstadt (Old Town): Staying in the Altstadt provides proximity to major attractions like the Heidelberg Castle, museums, and the picturesque Old Town streets. Hotels and guesthouses here offer easy access to historic landmarks, charming cafés, and shopping districts.

Neckar Riverfront: Accommodations along the Neckar River offer scenic views and a tranquil ambiance. This area is perfect for those seeking a peaceful retreat while being within walking distance of the city center and its attractions.

Bergheim: Known for its vibrant atmosphere, Bergheim is a lively district filled with trendy cafés, bars, and cultural spots. It's an excellent choice for those interested in exploring Heidelberg's contemporary art scene and nightlife.

Budget-Friendly vs. Luxury Stays: Finding the Perfect Accommodation

Budget-Friendly Options: Travelers seeking budget-friendly accommodations can find affordable guesthouses, hostels, or smaller hotels slightly away from the city center. Consider accommodations in the Bergheim district or along public transport routes for more economical stays without compromising on comfort.

Luxury Stays: For those seeking luxury and indulgence, opt for upscale hotels or boutique establishments nestled within the Old Town or overlooking the Neckar River. These accommodations offer lavish amenities, exceptional service, and breathtaking views, ensuring an opulent and memorable experience.

When choosing accommodation in Heidelberg, consider your preferences, budget, and desired experiences. Whether it's the historical charm of the Old Town, the tranquility of riverside stays, or the vibrancy of cultural districts, Heidelberg offers a plethora of accommodation options to cater to diverse traveler needs and preferences.

This overview aims to guide travelers in selecting accommodation in Heidelberg by outlining various types of stays, highlighting neighborhood insights, and providing considerations for both budget-friendly and luxury accommodations, ensuring a comfortable and enjoyable stay in the city.

Chapter 5: Outdoor Activities and Day Trips

Hiking and Nature Trails Around Heidelberg

Heidelberg is surrounded by picturesque landscapes, offering an array of hiking and nature trails that cater to outdoor enthusiasts of all skill levels.

Philosophers' Walk (Philosophenweg): This renowned trail is a must-visit, offering breathtaking views of Heidelberg's Old Town and the Neckar River valley. Accessible from the Old Bridge, the Philosophers' Walk winds through vineyards and lush greenery, providing a serene escape and an opportunity for contemplation, just as it did for scholars and philosophers centuries ago.

Heiligenberg and Michaelskloster: Embark on a hike to Heiligenberg, the "Holy Mountain," which houses the ruins of Michaelskloster, a former monastery. The trail through the forested slopes leads to scenic viewpoints overlooking Heidelberg, the castle, and the surrounding landscape. It's an ideal route for nature lovers and history buffs alike.

Königstuhl and Felsenmeer: For a more challenging hike, venture to Königstuhl, the highest hill in the vicinity, and explore the Felsenmeer (Sea of Rocks), a unique geological formation. Traversing through wooded paths and stunning rock formations, this trail offers an adventurous experience and unparalleled vistas of the Rhine Valley.

Day Trips from Heidelberg: Nearby Towns and Attractions

Schwetzingen: Just a short journey from Heidelberg lies Schwetzingen, renowned for its splendid Schwetzingen Palace and Gardens. Explore the meticulously landscaped gardens, adorned with sculptures, fountains, and exotic flora, offering a glimpse into 18th-century aristocratic life.

Ladenburg: Steeped in history, Ladenburg is a charming town with well-preserved medieval architecture. Visit the Romanesque Market Square, the Carl Benz Museum showcasing the history of automobiles, and the ancient Jewish mikveh (ritual bath), reflecting the town's rich heritage.

Speyer: Approximately an hour away, Speyer boasts the UNESCO-listed Speyer Cathedral, a masterpiece of Romanesque architecture. The Historical Museum of the Palatinate offers insight into regional history, while Technik Museum Speyer displays aircraft, vintage cars, and a space shuttle.

Neckar Valley: Cruise along the scenic Neckar Valley by boat or rent a bike to explore the picturesque towns along the river. Stop by Neckarsteinach, known for its four medieval castles, or visit the quaint town of Neckargemünd, offering idyllic riverside views and historical charm.

Baden-Baden: A slightly longer day trip takes you to Baden-Baden, a spa town renowned for its thermal baths, elegant architecture, and the opulent Baden-Baden Casino. Stroll through the beautifully manicured Lichtentaler Allee, or visit the renowned Museum Frieder Burda for its impressive art collection.

Heidelberg's surroundings offer a myriad of outdoor activities, from serene nature trails to enriching day trips to neighboring towns and attractions. Whether hiking through verdant landscapes, exploring historical sites, or immersing in the charm of nearby towns, these experiences promise to add depth and diversity to your exploration beyond Heidelberg's city limits.

Cycling Adventures and Vineyard Tours

Neckar Valley Cycling Path: Cycling enthusiasts can embark on a scenic journey along the Neckar River, traversing through charming towns, verdant vineyards, and enchanting landscapes. The well-maintained cycling paths offer a leisurely way to explore the region, with opportunities to stop at local wineries for tastings or simply relish the serene beauty of the valley.

Mountain Biking Trails: For more adventurous souls, the surrounding hillsides and forests present thrilling mountain biking trails. Trails around Königstuhl or the Odenwald region offer diverse terrains, from challenging single tracks to leisurely routes, catering to varying skill levels amidst picturesque natural settings.

Historical Excursions and Cultural Explorations

Mannheim: A short trip from Heidelberg takes you to Mannheim, known for its Baroque Palace, one of the largest in Europe. Explore the vast palace grounds, visit the Technoseum to discover industrial history, or simply stroll through the lively city center.

Wiesloch and Walldorf: Explore the towns of Wiesloch and Walldorf, known for their historical significance as the birthplace of the automobile. Visit the Benz-Daimler-Halle, commemorating the invention of the first car, and discover automotive history at the Motorwelt Museum.

Eberbach Abbey: Venture to the Eberbach Abbey, a magnificent former Cistercian monastery set amidst the picturesque Rheingau region. Explore the well-preserved abbey, take guided tours, and delve into the history and winemaking heritage of the area.

Outdoor Adventure Parks and Recreational Escapes

Hockenheimring: Motorsport enthusiasts might opt for a trip to Hockenheim, home to the famous Hockenheimring race track. Attend thrilling racing events or visit the Motor-Sport-Museum Hockenheim to delve into the world of motorsports.

Outdoor Adventure Parks: Families and thrill-seekers can head to adventure parks like Holiday Park or Kurpfalz-Park for an adrenaline-filled day with rides, wildlife encounters, and outdoor activities amidst beautiful natural settings, perfect for a fun-filled day trip.

Nature Reserves and Natural Wonders

Odenwald Nature Park: Embark on an exploration of Odenwald Nature Park, offering a sanctuary for hikers, cyclists, and nature lovers. Discover diverse flora and fauna, explore tranquil forests, and relish panoramic views from scenic viewpoints.

Dr. Carl Benz Nature Trail: Follow the Dr. Carl Benz Nature Trail, an educational and scenic hiking trail that combines nature exploration with insights into the life and work of Carl Benz, the inventor of the automobile, offering an interactive experience amidst nature.

Boat Excursions and River Adventures

Neckar River Cruises: Consider extending your exploration of the Neckar River by taking leisurely boat excursions. These cruises offer a relaxed way to soak in the scenic beauty, passing through charming villages, vineyards, and historical landmarks while enjoying informative commentary about the region's history and culture.

Kayaking and Canoeing: Embrace an active water adventure by renting kayaks or canoes to paddle along the Neckar River. This hands-on experience allows for an up-close encounter with nature and the surrounding landscapes, offering a different perspective of Heidelberg's beauty.

Quaint Villages and Historical Enclaves
Eltville am Rhein: Journey towards the Rhine Valley to visit Eltville, a picturesque town famous for its wine culture. Explore the historic town center, stroll through vineyards, and visit medieval castles like Burg Eltville while savoring the region's renowned Riesling wines.

Eberstadt and Zwingenberg: Discover the charm of Eberstadt and Zwingenberg, quaint villages nestled amidst the Bergstraße wine region. Wander through vineyard-covered hills, explore historic churches, and enjoy wine tastings in traditional cellars, immersing yourself in the local winemaking heritage.

Cultural Heritage Sites and Artistic Landscapes

Würzburg: Venture further afield to Würzburg, a city famous for its baroque architecture and the UNESCO-listed Würzburg Residence. Explore the opulent palace and its splendid gardens, visit the Marienberg Fortress, and stroll along the scenic Alte Mainbrücke (Old Main Bridge).

Lorsch Abbey: Step back in time by visiting Lorsch Abbey, a UNESCO World Heritage Site showcasing Carolingian architecture. Wander through the remnants of the abbey complex, including the impressive gatehouse, cloister, and the Königshalle (King's Hall), reflecting the region's medieval history.

Educational and Science-Infused Excursions

Technik Museum Sinsheim: For enthusiasts of technology and aviation, consider a day trip to the

Technik Museum Sinsheim. Explore an extensive collection of aircraft, vintage cars, locomotives, and even a supersonic Concorde, offering a fascinating insight into the world of transportation and technology.

German Cancer Research Center (DKFZ): Engage in an educational tour at the German Cancer Research Center in Heidelberg. The center offers informative exhibitions and guided tours, providing insights into cancer research, innovations in healthcare, and the center's groundbreaking contributions to science.

Chapter 6: Shopping and Local Experiences

Heidelberg's Shopping Scene: Souvenirs and Local Crafts

Altstadt Boutiques and Shops: Heidelberg's Old Town (Altstadt) is a shopper's paradise, boasting an eclectic mix of boutiques, artisanal shops, and souvenir stores lining the cobblestone streets. Discover unique souvenirs like traditional beer steins, handmade cuckoo clocks, and intricate wood carvings that encapsulate the city's heritage.

Marktplatz Market Stalls: Visit the bustling Marktplatz, where vendors showcase an array of local products and crafts. From handmade ceramics to locally produced honey, jams, and chocolates, the market stalls offer a treasure trove of authentic Heidelberg goods, perfect for memorable gifts or personal keepsakes.

Schlosshof Passage: Explore the Schlosshof Passage near Heidelberg Castle, home to a collection of artisan workshops and specialty stores. Delight in handcrafted jewelry, leather goods, and artistic creations produced by local craftsmen, providing a glimpse into Heidelberg's thriving arts scene.

Unique Experiences: Workshops and Cultural Immersions

Artisan Workshops: Immerse yourself in hands-on experiences by joining workshops conducted by local artisans. Engage in pottery classes, glassblowing sessions, or painting workshops, where skilled craftsmen share their expertise, allowing you to create personalized mementos infused with Heidelberg's artistic flair.

Culinary Adventures: Delve into the region's gastronomic heritage through culinary workshops and tastings. Learn the art of pretzel making, participate in wine-tasting sessions at local vineyards, or attend cooking classes to master traditional German dishes, enhancing your connection to Heidelberg's culinary traditions.

Language and Cultural Exchanges: Engage with the locals through language exchange meetups or cultural immersion programs. Participate in language classes, cultural seminars, or guided tours led by enthusiastic locals, offering insights into Heidelberg's history, customs, and way of life.

Artisanal Crafts and Hidden Gems

Heidelberg Artisan Markets: Attend artisan markets and craft fairs that periodically take place across Heidelberg. These events showcase the talents of local artists, offering a diverse selection of handmade goods, from textiles and ceramics to intricate woodwork and innovative artworks.

Hidden Boutiques and Art Galleries: Explore off-the-beaten-path boutiques and art galleries scattered throughout Heidelberg. Wander into hidden alleys to discover artistic treasures, contemporary artworks, and unique crafts that often go unnoticed by casual visitors, providing an opportunity to acquire exclusive pieces.

Cultural Immersions and Authentic Encounters

Local Festivals and Cultural Celebrations: Immerse yourself in Heidelberg's vibrant cultural scene by attending local festivals and events. From the

Heidelberg Spring Festival to traditional Christmas markets, these celebrations offer a platform to interact with locals, partake in age-old traditions, and sample regional specialties.

Traditional Crafts Demonstrations: Seek out venues hosting demonstrations of traditional crafts, such as blacksmithing, bookbinding, or fabric weaving. These demonstrations not only showcase age-old techniques but also offer a chance to engage with artisans and gain a deeper appreciation for their craftsmanship.

Heidelberg's shopping scene extends beyond traditional souvenir hunting, offering a plethora of unique experiences, workshops, artisan crafts, and cultural immersions. Whether exploring charming boutiques in the Old Town, engaging in hands-on workshops, or immersing oneself in the city's cultural fabric, these experiences provide a deeper understanding of Heidelberg's rich heritage and a chance to take home cherished mementos infused with local craftsmanship and cultural significance.

Vintage Finds and Antique Markets

Antique Shops and Flea Markets: Explore Heidelberg's antique shops and flea markets, where hidden treasures await discovery. From vintage postcards and historic memorabilia to classic vinyl records and retro clothing, these markets offer a nostalgic journey into the past.

Friedrich-Ebert-Platz Flea Market: Visit the Friedrich-Ebert-Platz Flea Market, a beloved spot for antique enthusiasts and collectors. Browse through stalls selling unique items like old books, collectible coins, vintage toys, and eclectic artifacts, perfect for those seeking one-of-a-kind souvenirs.

Local Experiences and Hands-on Learning

Traditional Music and Instrument Workshops: Immerse yourself in Heidelberg's musical heritage by participating in traditional music workshops. Learn to play regional instruments like the zither or participate in folk music sessions, immersing yourself in the city's rich musical traditions.

Join Local Art Clubs or Studios: Engage with Heidelberg's artistic community by joining local art clubs or studios. Participate in painting classes, sculpture workshops, or photography groups, fostering creative exchanges and allowing you to interact with passionate local artists.

Cultural Performances and Theatrical Experiences
Local Theater Productions: Attend local theater productions showcasing Heidelberg's vibrant performing arts scene. From classic plays to contemporary performances, these shows provide a glimpse into the city's theatrical culture and offer a chance to support local talent.

Street Performances and Cultural Festivals: Keep an eye out for street performances and impromptu displays during cultural festivals or special events. These spontaneous showcases of music, dance, and street art add vibrancy to the city's atmosphere, providing delightful encounters for passersby.

Artistic Workshops and Craft Markets
Art and Craft Fairs: Explore craft markets and art fairs that intermittently take place in Heidelberg. These events gather local artisans, showcasing handmade jewelry, textiles, ceramics, and innovative

artworks, providing a platform for unique artistic encounters.

Artistic Workshops for Children and Families: Look for workshops tailored for families and children, offering creative activities like pottery painting, DIY crafts, or storytelling sessions. These workshops foster a love for arts and crafts while creating enjoyable experiences for families exploring Heidelberg together.

Specialty Food and Culinary Workshops

Local Food Tastings and Workshops: Indulge in local food tastings or workshops focusing on regional delicacies. From chocolate tastings to cheese-making classes or beer brewing workshops, these culinary experiences immerse participants in Heidelberg's gastronomic heritage.

Market Tours and Cooking Classes: Join guided market tours followed by cooking classes that showcase traditional German recipes. Engage in market-to-table experiences, selecting fresh produce and learning to prepare authentic dishes under the guidance of local chefs.

Artistic Residencies and Cultural Exchanges

Artist Residencies: Explore artist residencies or creative spaces that occasionally host artists-in-residence programs. These venues often organize open studio events or exhibitions, allowing visitors to interact with artists, witness their creative process, and acquire original artworks directly from the creators.

Cultural Exchange Programs: Seek out cultural exchange programs that facilitate interactions between travelers and locals. Participate in language exchange meetups, cultural workshops, or community-driven initiatives, fostering cross-cultural dialogues and fostering meaningful connections.

Hidden Gems and Local Haunts

Offbeat Stores and Niche Boutiques: Delve into Heidelberg's hidden gems, including specialty stores and niche boutiques tucked away in lesser-known corners. Discover unconventional items, from handcrafted leather goods and unique fashion pieces to quirky home décor, offering distinctive souvenirs beyond the mainstream offerings.

Local Bookstores and Literary Events: Explore local bookstores or attend literary events that celebrate Heidelberg's literary heritage. Engage in book readings, author signings, or join book clubs discussing works associated with the city, fostering a deeper appreciation for its literary contributions.

Community Workshops and Volunteering Opportunities

Community Workshops and Initiatives: Look for community-driven workshops or initiatives that aim to preserve local traditions or support social causes. Participate in community art projects, sustainability workshops, or volunteer for initiatives contributing to Heidelberg's cultural and environmental welfare.

Nature Conservation and Eco-Tours: Engage in eco-friendly experiences like nature conservation programs or guided eco-tours focusing on sustainable practices. Participate in tree planting activities, nature walks led by conservationists, or educational tours highlighting environmental conservation efforts in the region.

Interactive Cultural Heritage Sites

Living History Exhibits: Experience living history exhibits or open-air museums showcasing Heidelberg's past. Interact with costumed interpreters portraying historical figures, engage in traditional crafts demonstrations, and immerse yourself in bygone eras brought to life.

Themed Tours and Guided Walks: Opt for themed tours or guided walks that explore specific facets of Heidelberg's history and culture. From ghost tours delving into local legends to architectural walks highlighting iconic buildings, these tours offer intriguing insights and unique perspectives.

Heidelberg's offerings extend far beyond conventional shopping experiences, providing a myriad of opportunities for deep immersion, artistic engagements, community involvement, and cultural exploration. These hidden gems, artistic exchanges, and interactive experiences allow travelers to forge authentic connections with Heidelberg's heritage, arts, and local communities, fostering enriching and meaningful experiences.

Chapter 7: Practical Tips and Resources

Transportation in Heidelberg: Getting Around the City

Public Transport: Heidelberg boasts an efficient public transportation system comprising trams, buses, and trains. The extensive network connects the city's various districts, making it convenient for travelers to explore. Consider purchasing a HeidelbergCARD for unlimited travel on public transport and discounted entry to attractions.

Walking and Cycling: Heidelberg's compact size and pedestrian-friendly layout make walking an excellent way to navigate the city center. Many areas are cyclist-friendly too, offering bike rentals for those keen on exploring Heidelberg's charming streets and scenic riverside paths on two wheels.

Taxi Services: Taxis are readily available in Heidelberg and are a convenient option, especially for late-night travels or reaching destinations not easily accessible by public transport. Reliable taxi services can be hailed from designated taxi stands or booked through apps.

Useful Phrases and Language Tips

Common Phrases: Learning a few basic German phrases can greatly enhance your experience in Heidelberg. Useful phrases include greetings (Guten Tag - Good day), courtesy phrases (Bitte - Please, Danke - Thank you), and simple questions (Sprechen Sie Englisch? - Do you speak English?).

Language Apps and Guides: Consider downloading language apps like Duolingo or carrying pocket-sized phrasebooks for quick reference. These resources aid in learning essential phrases, improving communication, and showcasing cultural respect by attempting the local language.

Engaging Locals: Even if most locals speak English, attempting to converse in German is appreciated and fosters a friendlier interaction. Locals often respond positively to visitors trying to communicate in their language, creating a more immersive experience.

Safety Precautions and Emergency Contacts

General Safety: Heidelberg is relatively safe, but it's essential to practice general safety precautions. Be mindful of your belongings in crowded areas and avoid displaying valuables openly. Emergency services like police (Polizei), ambulance (Krankenwagen), and fire department (Feuerwehr) are accessible by dialing 112.

Healthcare and Medical Services: Heidelberg offers excellent medical facilities and pharmacies (Apotheke) for any health-related needs. EU citizens can access medical care using the European Health Insurance Card (EHIC). Non-EU travelers should have comprehensive travel insurance covering medical expenses.

Emergency Contacts: Apart from 112 for emergencies, note down local contacts such as the tourist information center, your country's embassy or consulate, and your accommodation's emergency contact number for quick assistance.

Local Resources and Information
Tourist Information Centers: Utilize the services provided by Heidelberg's tourist information centers

located in the city center and at major transportation hubs. They offer maps, brochures, guidance on attractions, and assistance in multiple languages.

Mobile Apps and Online Resources: Numerous mobile apps and online resources provide real-time information on transportation schedules, city maps, and attractions. Apps like Moovit and Google Maps are handy for navigating public transport routes and timetables.

Local Events and Festivals: Stay updated on local events, festivals, and cultural happenings by checking event calendars, city websites, or following social media accounts of Heidelberg's tourism boards. Participating in these events offers insights into the city's culture and traditions.

Mastering transportation, embracing basic language skills, prioritizing safety, and accessing local resources are crucial aspects of a smooth and enjoyable stay in Heidelberg. Equipping oneself with these practical tips and resources enhances the overall travel experience, ensuring a seamless exploration of the city while fostering cultural understanding and safety awareness.

Local Customs and Etiquette

Greetings and Etiquette: Germans appreciate formalities in greetings. Use titles such as Herr (Mr.) or Frau (Mrs./Ms.) with the surname when addressing someone until invited to use first names. A firm handshake and direct eye contact are customary during introductions.

Dining Etiquette: When dining out, it's customary to wait until everyone is served before starting the meal. Don't place your elbows on the table, and remember to say "Prost" (cheers) when clinking glasses during a toast.

Punctuality and Respect: Germans highly value punctuality, so be on time for appointments, tours, or reservations. Respect personal space and privacy, maintaining a moderate volume in public spaces.

Navigating Cultural Differences

Cash vs. Cards: While credit cards are widely accepted, smaller businesses, street vendors, and markets might prefer cash payments. Have some euros on hand for these situations, and keep your credit card PIN handy as some transactions may require it.

Shopping Hours: Shops in Heidelberg typically open from around 9 AM to 8 PM on weekdays, with shorter hours on Saturdays and limited hours on Sundays. Plan shopping excursions accordingly, especially if looking for specific items or gifts.

Waste Management: Heidelberg practices strict waste separation. Familiarize yourself with the different bins for recyclables, compost, and general waste to ensure proper disposal during your stay.

Adapting to Local Lifestyle

Relaxation and Leisure: Embrace the local pace of life by indulging in leisurely activities. Enjoy a coffee at a café, take scenic walks along the river, or simply sit back and absorb the atmosphere at one of the city's beautiful squares.

Seasonal Considerations: Heidelberg experiences distinct seasons. Be prepared for weather changes – pack accordingly for warm summers, cool winters, and potentially rainy days. Check weather forecasts before planning outdoor activities.

Cultural Sensitivity: Be mindful of cultural sensitivities and local customs. Avoid discussing sensitive historical topics unless engaged by locals and be respectful when visiting religious sites or during cultural events.

Engaging with Local Communities

Community Participation: Consider engaging in volunteer opportunities or community projects during your stay. Local organizations often welcome volunteers for various activities, providing opportunities for meaningful interactions and cultural exchanges.

Local Culinary Experiences: Attend food festivals, cooking workshops, or dine at local eateries to savor authentic regional cuisine. Engaging with local food traditions enhances cultural understanding and allows you to experience Heidelberg's culinary diversity.

Arts and Crafts Experiences: Participate in art exhibitions, craft workshops, or visit artist studios to support the local creative community. Purchasing locally made crafts directly from artisans promotes their craftsmanship and contributes to the city's cultural vibrancy.

Health and Well-being

Medical Services for Tourists: Familiarize yourself with the locations of hospitals, clinics, and pharmacies in Heidelberg. It's wise to carry essential medications, especially if you have specific health needs, and have a copy of your prescriptions for reference.

Water Safety: Tap water in Heidelberg is safe for drinking. Carry a refillable water bottle to stay hydrated while exploring the city. Refilling stations are available in various public areas, reducing the need for single-use plastic bottles.

Technology and Connectivity

Mobile Connectivity: Ensure your mobile phone is compatible with local networks or consider purchasing a local SIM card for reliable connectivity during your stay. Free Wi-Fi is available at many cafés, restaurants, and public spaces in Heidelberg.

Travel Apps and Maps: Besides transportation apps, download city maps or offline maps to navigate Heidelberg, especially in areas with limited connectivity. These resources help you find attractions, restaurants, and amenities offline.

Respecting Heritage Sites and Cultural Sites

Heritage Site Etiquette: When visiting historical or religious sites, adhere to guidelines and regulations. Respect signage, avoid littering, and refrain from disruptive behavior to preserve the sanctity and integrity of these places.

Photography Rules: While photography is generally allowed in most places, some sites may have restrictions or require permits for professional photography. Observe rules about flash photography, tripod usage, and respect privacy if photographing people.

Local Cuisine and Dining Etiquette

Tipping Practices: Tipping in Germany is appreciated but not obligatory. It's customary to round up the bill or leave a 5-10% tip at restaurants or for exceptional service. Verify if service charges are already included in the bill.

Culinary Explorations: Venture beyond traditional restaurants and explore local markets or food stalls. Taste regional specialties like pretzels, bratwurst, and local cheeses, or indulge in culinary tours to experience diverse flavors.

Environmentally Conscious Travel

Sustainable Choices: Practice eco-friendly travel by opting for reusable items, minimizing plastic use, and supporting eco-conscious businesses. Look for green accommodations and participate in initiatives supporting environmental conservation.

Responsible Tourism: Be mindful of your impact on the environment and local communities. Respect nature trails, follow designated paths, and refrain from littering or damaging natural habitats.

Mastering practical aspects such as health considerations, connectivity, respecting cultural sites, and environmental awareness enhances your overall experience in Heidelberg. These additional tips encompass various aspects, ensuring a smoother and more culturally enriching journey while respecting local customs and preserving the city's heritage and environment.

Exploration Beyond Tourist Hotspots

Off-the-Beaten-Path Experiences: Explore neighborhoods and areas less frequented by tourists. Engage with locals in community events, visit neighborhood markets, or discover hidden gems to gain a more authentic understanding of daily life in Heidelberg.

Local Hangouts: Venture to local cafes, pubs, and eateries frequented by residents. Engaging in conversations with locals can provide invaluable insights into their culture, lifestyle, and even recommendations for lesser-known attractions.

Cultural Understanding and Interactions

Cultural Sensitivity: Learn about cultural norms and traditions to show respect during interactions. Understanding social customs and gestures helps foster positive exchanges and avoids unintentional misunderstandings.

Appreciating Diversity: Heidelberg is a multicultural city with a diverse population. Embrace and celebrate this diversity by engaging in events or activities that highlight different cultural influences within the city.

Supporting Local Businesses and Artisans

Artisanal Discoveries: Seek out local artisans, craftsmen, and independent businesses to support the local economy. Purchasing handmade goods or artworks directly from artisans not only aids local livelihoods but also offers unique and meaningful souvenirs.

Farmers' Markets and Local Produce: Explore farmers' markets to sample fresh produce, locally sourced goods, and artisanal products. Contributing to the local economy by purchasing directly from producers promotes sustainable practices and connects you with authentic regional flavors.

Immersion in Cultural Celebrations

Participation in Festivals: Plan your visit during local festivals or cultural celebrations to experience Heidelberg's vibrant spirit. Engaging in festivities allows for a firsthand experience of local traditions, music, dance, and cuisine.

Traditional Customs and Rituals: Learn about and participate in traditional customs or rituals, such as seasonal festivals or religious ceremonies. Respectfully engaging with these practices provides a deeper understanding of the city's cultural tapestry.

Engaging in Educational Pursuits

Museums and Educational Centers: Heidelberg is home to various museums and educational centers. Attend lectures, workshops, or exhibitions that delve into the city's history, art, science, or literature to broaden your understanding of its cultural legacy.

University Engagements: Take advantage of Heidelberg's renowned university by attending public lectures, academic discussions, or campus events. Engaging with the academic community offers insights into diverse fields of study and intellectual discourse.

Exploring Heidelberg goes beyond typical sightseeing; it involves immersing oneself in local life, supporting artisans and businesses, appreciating cultural diversity, and embracing educational opportunities. Engaging with the city on multiple levels enriches the travel experience and fosters a deeper connection with Heidelberg's heritage, people, and cultural nuances.

Conclusion

Reflections on Heidelberg's Timeless Beauty

Historic Enchantment: Heidelberg, nestled along the Neckar River, embodies a blend of historical allure and modern vitality. The city's cobblestone streets, well-preserved architecture, and the majestic Heidelberg Castle overlooking the Altstadt evoke a timeless ambiance, drawing visitors into its enchanting embrace.

Riverside Splendor: The serene Neckar River, flanked by lush greenery and punctuated by charming bridges, creates a picturesque setting. Riverside walks, cruises, and the idyllic Philosophers' Walk offer glimpses of Heidelberg's tranquil beauty, captivating travelers with their scenic vistas.

Cultural Richness: Heidelberg's cultural heritage, epitomized by its renowned university, vibrant arts scene, and diverse festivals, infuses the city with a vibrant energy. Museums, theaters, and a thriving culinary scene contribute to an immersive experience, revealing the city's multifaceted cultural tapestry.

Natural Charms: Beyond its urban allure, Heidelberg boasts natural splendors. The surrounding hills, vineyard-draped landscapes, and the nearby Odenwald Forest offer outdoor enthusiasts hiking trails, panoramic views, and an escape into nature's embrace just a stone's throw from the city center.

Tips for Sustainable Travel in Heidelberg

Responsible Accommodation Choices: Opt for eco-friendly accommodations committed to sustainability practices. Consider eco-certified hotels, guesthouses employing green initiatives, or staying in locally owned accommodations that support the community.

Reduce Plastic Usage: Minimize single-use plastic consumption by carrying a reusable water bottle, eco-friendly shopping bags, and utensils. Refill stations for water bottles are available across the city, reducing the need for disposable plastic bottles.

Public Transport and Cycling: Embrace the city's efficient public transport system, utilizing trams, buses, and trains to reduce carbon emissions. Alternatively, explore Heidelberg on foot or by renting bicycles, contributing to a greener environment while immersing yourself in the city's charm.

Support Local and Sustainable Businesses: Patronize local eateries serving seasonal, locally sourced produce and support farmers' markets. Choose restaurants or cafés committed to sustainable practices, reducing food miles and promoting a farm-to-table dining experience.

Respect Cultural and Environmental Heritage: Honor the city's heritage by respecting historical sites, cultural norms, and natural environments. Follow designated trails, obey regulations at heritage sites, and participate in organized eco-tours that promote responsible exploration.

Waste Management and Recycling: Embrace the city's waste separation practices by disposing of trash in designated bins. Familiarize yourself with recycling guidelines to properly sort recyclables, contributing to Heidelberg's commitment to environmental conservation.

Preserving Heidelberg's Legacy for Future Generations

Heidelberg's enduring appeal lies not only in its architectural marvels or scenic landscapes but also in the collective effort to safeguard its cultural legacy and natural beauty for generations to come. Sustainable travel practices play a pivotal role in preserving this legacy, ensuring that the city remains a cherished destination for years to come.

By adopting eco-conscious behaviors, supporting local initiatives, and respecting Heidelberg's cultural and environmental heritage, travelers can actively contribute to the city's sustainable future. The convergence of responsible travel practices and appreciation for Heidelberg's timeless allure ensures a harmonious coexistence between visitors, locals, and the city's rich history.

Heidelberg's allure transcends time, inviting travelers to immerse themselves in its historical splendor, cultural vibrancy, and natural wonders.

Embracing sustainable travel practices while exploring this enchanting city ensures that future generations can continue to cherish and revel in the timeless beauty that Heidelberg so graciously embodies.

Printed in Great Britain
by Amazon

39473882R00046